# Thanks To America
## Against All Odds

*Follow Your [signature] dreams*

*Aug 15, 2010*

D1002509

## By Joseph Golshani

Outskirts Press, Inc.
Denver, Colorado

Outskirts Press, Inc.
http://www.outskirtspress.com

ISBN: 978-1-4327-2510-5

Outskirts Press and the "OP" logo are trademarks belonging to Outskirts Press, Inc.

PRINTED IN THE UNITED STATES OF AMERICA

To my wife, Behnaz, and my loving children, Nika and Bijan, who I am very proud of.

# Contents

# Acknowledgements

I want to thank everyone who encouraged me to write this book. Most notably to my wife, Behnaz, who, for over twenty years, has been my support through the success and the good times, and a few bad times too.

Thanks to my daughter, Nika, and my son, Bijan, for being such great kids. Thanks to my mother and father who, without their love and support, this would not have happened. Thanks Mom for all your wonderful advice and hard work after coming to America and becoming financially independent even though our father did not like it. And, you did it with broken English. To my brothers, Parviz, Nasser, Amir, and Shahriyar, who have always been there when I needed them, and my sister, Shohreh, and her husband, Said. And to my extended family, especially my brother-in-law, Madjid, and his wife, Mechelle, who helped me in the beginning of my career, and my mother-in-law, Raffat.

Special thanks go to the following people and companies for their continued friendship, encouragement, and support: Roya and Kamy Deljou, Jim and Delores Ellis, Shahzad and Fariba Haddadi, Sima and Mohamad Sedehe, I.J. Rosenberg, the folks at Security Bank, the Neill Corporation, the Aveda Corporation, and Pardis Publications. Thanks also to Jerry Braxton, Brad Hess, Tom Waldon, Drew Grizzard, Gary Mastrogiovanni, Lin Rogers, Fay Dumke, George Pratte, and Bill Pretyman, who have been long-time clients for over twenty years.

Last but not least, thanks to all my team members, educational team, and management for their long hours of hard work and support of my vision.

And to those who I may have forgotten, those I know now, or will know in the future, or who I never had the chance to meet.

# Introduction

I, Khosrow Vossough Golshani, also known as Khosie, Joe, Joey or Joseph Golshani, was born in Tehran, Iran, on October 7, 1957, in a middle-class family with four brothers and one sister. My reason for writing this book is to share the thirty-plus years of experience and wisdom I gained coming from Iran to America. It is my tale of how America helped me grow physically, spiritually, and financially, far beyond my own imagination. It is what I believe I owe to America and to those traveling the same path. It is the thanks for my success.

As I tell my story, I will share with you the wisdom I was fortunate to learn from those who taught me along the way. People that were kind enough to share insights from their own lives, which helped me further my success. I will also attempt to convey my philosophy about life and how it can help you in your goals, no matter who or where you are. Goals are dreams, and I believe that if you truly want something, believe in it and dream it, and when the time is right, your goal will come true.

Writing this book was a goal of mine for many years, and when the time was right, the people that would eventually help me complete my goal came into my life at just the right time. I believe these people were meant to be there for me. We are an assemblage of people whose lives are linked together in a beautifully abstract way. I am Muslim, and my ghostwriter lost her husband on September 11, 2001, and my friend who helped provide the editing, artwork, and support is Jewish. It's a statement attesting to the fact that in America we are all equals. We see each other as people first and foremost.

I hope this book will be an inspiration to those who are here in the United States now, or who will be here in the future looking for their success. I want to show how any average person can make it in America. Maybe this book will give them the push they need to become who they want to be. God bless you, God bless America, and God bless the World.

# Chapter 1
## Inspiration

"It is not for him to pride himself who loveth his own country, but rather for him who loveth the whole world. The earth is but one country and mankind its citizens."

-Baha'u'llah

The idea of writing a book was probably one of the last, and scariest, things on my mind. First, I didn't think I could write very well and, second, I am not able to type at all. I thought that anyone writing a book needs to at least know that. But I discovered I was wrong when I met my ghostwriter, Barbara. What is interesting is that Barbara can read my handwriting even though I was told many times what horrible handwriting I have. By her continuous support she gave me the confidence to explain my ideas more freely, and to keep my focus on telling my story as it has happened, while not getting off the subject.

The idea of this book came about a couple of years ago while I was attending a seminar called Serious Business®, which is held every year in New Orleans by the Neill Corporation. One of the speakers was a man named Ray Civello, a very successful salon owner and businessman from Canada. He began his presentation by sharing a biographical story clip from his life. Afterward, he came onto the stage and asked the audience, "What is your story?" This put the seed in my head. What is my story? Really, what *is* my story? The more I thought about it the more I became interested in writing it. Since I don't like novels or fiction, I thought focusing on things that are real and things that I have personally experienced and been personally responsible for would be a great way to start. The more I thought about it, the more I became interested in the book idea. What a great way to leave something behind for my kids, especially something for them to share with their kids and the next generation to come.

I feel my story is very simple and not sophisticated at all. Throughout this book you will read about a simple philosophy I use in my everyday life, and how I mix the best ideas from both my Iranian and American cultures. And, because in America I am free to mix these good ideas from both cultures, it gives me the pleasure of publically and officially thanking America. I hope that I might start a trend among everyone who came to America from abroad and became successful. I hope that they will share their success stories in order to pave the way for the next generation.

Why "Against All Odds"? Because I am originally from Iran, and America is unfairly hated abroad and *supposedly* responsible for most everything, I find it odd that I have one of the top five salons in Atlanta and top fifty in America. It feels odd to be respected. I think it is odd some people think that I am odd. There are many reasons that I defy the odds, but what I am thankful for is that no matter how many reasons come my way from the past or in the future, I know that I have a great life in America and I love it. Through the American culture and its system, I have gained tremendous confidence in who I am and where I am from, and I can say that I am a proud Iranian-American citizen who has lived the American dream.

I have to admit, I was sometimes hesitant about writing this book because of concerns about what some people's reactions could be. But my fears made me realize I am doing this for myself, first and foremost, as well as for all those who have similar circumstances. It is coming from my heart, and when something comes from the heart, it will always shine through and leave a lasting impression. I like to think everybody is right as long as they don't try to make me or others believe that they are right or wrong.

In addition, I would like this book to be inspirational to every American citizen who is not happy here. Yes, this country might have its flaws; after all, we know nothing is perfect. But what could make it perfect is all of us doing the right things. I feel if I made it, so can anybody else, especially if you were born here with so much opportunity at your footsteps. Get up and just do it. To all of you who live in this great country, no matter where you are from, appreciate this great land and be who you want to be. Through hard work and persistence, anything is possible.

One of the reasons I appreciate America so much is it has helped me become more confident as my journey continues. I know there are people like me that share the same past experience; always looking over their shoulders, wondering if what they have could be taken away at any moment. Not sure if what they have is real. For me to be able to grow, I had to come to America. For someone else it could be another place. Perhaps there is something like America for everybody somewhere, and if there's not, let's try to make everywhere like America.

I have realized that a great quality of most successful people is their ability to recognize those who have helped them along the way in achieving their success, while also helping them to achieve their own. Since I am very fortunate to know people from all over the world, and also having served people through my profession as a salon owner and a hairdresser, I realized that so many people do not appreciate what a great place we have to live, and I wonder why they are not sharing their successes and being vocal about them. I hear too much about what America is not doing for them, and the fact that their country is not doing well is America's fault. What we should say is what am I doing for my country?

I like to say that my story is most likely a typical success story that has been happily occurring throughout the world by many successful individuals from all different backgrounds and cultures. But I would like to put this important question out to all those successful people: How many of you are willing to share your story with others? And why are you not sharing? After all, that is how we learn and benefit, by sharing. It is beautiful that our stories attract different audiences depending on the needs of each individual.

# Chapter 2
## In Need of Praise

"We don't receive wisdom; we must discover it for ourselves after a journey that no one can take for us or spare us."

-Marcel Proust

I came to America two years before the Iranian revolution. I have been back to Iran twice, once in 1993 and a second time in 1999. While the majority of my experience reflects the time before the revolution, I believe that a revolution does not change the culture of a country, the culture will always remain the same. I think it is the flexibility of the people of that country to be able to dance with every song that is played by any regime.

Geographically, Iran is a small version of the United States. It has beautiful beaches, lakes, mountains, rivers, and desert. And, over twenty-five hundred years of heritage. I am proud to say that I was an Iranian citizen. The capital of Iran is Tehran, and Tehran is a combination of many different American states. It has the capitol like Washington D.C., the traffic of New York, and the mountains of Utah. There are four seasons, and in the summer you can see snow on the mountain tops. In the city, it is very crowded with one of the worst traffic problems in the world. If you look from a high-rise building down onto the traffic, you will notice a majority of the cars are not obeying the lines of traffic. Sometimes it looks like there are five lines of traffic while it is only a three-lane road. It could be lack of a system, or maybe it is just our culture. Living in America and getting a few tickets cured me, especially when I found out that I could not bribe my way out of them!

The day I was born, my mother's water broke prematurely so my parents decided to deliver me at home. I believe I am the only one in the family who was born at home. Maybe that is one of the reasons why I am such a homebody. I have four brothers and one sister. My mom had been married once before and divorced, and had a son, Amir. My dad had been married before, but did not get divorced, and also had a son, Parviz. I know it is a little different, but we all had a great relationship in spite of all that. I believe that since my dad wanted more children his first wife let him marry again, and my mom and dad had three sons and one daughter as a result: Nasser, Shahriyar, Shohreh, and me, after Nasser.

I had a great relationship with my dad's first wife, Aghdas, who I also called mom. She was a great mom, especially good at playing backgammon and playing cards, and she was a great cook as well. God bless her soul and be in peace. We miss you a lot, Mom. We all talk about how much fun you were.

My dad had just bought a house for Mom, but the house was outside of the city district and it did not have city water or power yet. My dad asked me to spend some time with Mom since my brother, Parviz, was in the army at the time. I was twelve years old, and I accepted since I liked her a lot. When I look back on my life now, I have a greater appreciation of that short summertime with Mom. Every day I had to walk about three miles to get drinking water and carry the heavy container back to her house. That sure made me a stronger kid, as did not having power or all the luxury items that I was used to at the time. And it made me better appreciate what I have now. What I know from that experience is that even though it was hard, I had great times, and it paved the road for who I am today.

I grew up in a middle class family in Iran. Being middle class has many advantages. I think it exposes you to both the lower and upper classes, and it sets you up for choosing which one you would rather be in, or deciding to just stay where you are. It helps you to connect much easier to any individual with any social background. For that same reason, I prefer public schools over private schools because I think they allow one to be exposed to much more of a variety of people. The main difference between social groups in America and what I was accustomed to in Iran is that in America I could do most anything and not be looked down upon by the other classes.

During this time in Iran, people watched American movies and dressed like those in the Western world. There was more freedom, maybe not a hundred percent, but I can say much more than now. They drove American cars, too. My father's first car was a big black Chrysler. Our family and relatives were very close growing up, and we had some of the best vacations together. Weekends in Iran were only

Fridays because you went to school and worked six days a week, therefore, we had three months of summer to vacation. Iran has some of the best places to vacation. We went to the mountains and skied. And we had many family trips to the beach. We could swim together, as there were no restrictions like there are now. Today in Iran, women and men cannot swim together unless the women wear the scarves and clothing that will keep them completely covered. If a woman wants to swim in a bathing suit, she must swim in an area for women only where no men are around to see her.

I was born a Muslim. I prayed, I would fast, I practiced not lying and stealing, and I went to mosque, the Muslim house of worship. To this day, I still become enchanted when I hear the *Azaan*, a chant broadcast over loud speakers that is used to call all Muslims to prayer five times a day. I remember at an early age, I used to go to mosque and the cleric would be talking about the past. In order for privacy they would turn off the lights so the attendees would be able to cry in private. No matter how hard I tried I could never cry. So that I would not stand out in the crowd, I would wet my eyes with my saliva when they turned the lights up again. That bothered me. Why did I have to pretend that I had cried? I always wondered what percentage of the crowd was in the same shoes as I was. I am sure a lot. Pretending something that is not true, I believe, is not something that the Muslim religion teaches. I like to say more likely it was the system, or the clergymen who were not able to educate people like me so we could understand, or tell us it is okay if you don't feel like crying. That is a better way.

I had three older brothers growing up, and I lived in a society where it was known that the elders knew everything and everything had to be approved by them. Because of this I became very timid and shy, and I was not confident about myself. Since my older brother, Nasser, was involved in sports, I gravitated to sports as well. I never thought or believed I could be as good as he was, but I always tagged along, and in doing so I learned more from him as life went on.

In the first grade at school, I recall being told that I would not pass. My first-grade teacher told me at the end of the school year that I would be her guest again next year. Being young and naïve, I rushed home to tell my father what a great honor had been extended to me, that my teacher has only told me that I will be her guest again next year. My father smiled and said, "That is great, son. Good job." My parents agreed I should repeat the first grade. The lesson I learned was sometimes it is okay to go with the flow. It will be okay as long as you know what is right and wrong. But after that second year in the first grade, I was again held back. My father was a member of the PTA and he convinced the school to move me up into the second grade. But, again, I did not pass and was held back. My father tried to convince the school a second time to move me up. He was worried about the embarrassment it would cause me and our family.

My parents consulted with a doctor to find out why I continued to fail. The doctor told them that I needed encouragement, and that I needed to be praised for my work. When my parents told this to the principle of my school he asked, "How can you reward someone for being bad?" But sometime later during the school year, my principle called me into his office. I had done something well and for that he gave me a gift. It was a pencil. There were other occasions where this was repeated as well. From the third grade on I did not fail again. The lesson I learned was that every flower blooms if it is taken care of.

# Chapter 3
## Coming to America

"The golden opportunity you are seeking is in yourself. It is not in your environment; it is not in luck or chance, or the help of others; it is in yourself alone."

-Orison Swett Marden

**W**hile growing up in Iran I was told that if you know how to speak English you will get a much better job. In Iran, as a result of the high demand for higher education, but a difficult school system, it was very hard to enter into university. You had to be really good to do so. I was an average student, and I was made to believe that I was average as a whole because of it. University in Iran, and the school system in Iran in general, has a high standard and you really have to study hard to enter into university. Because of the limited number of universities and the high demand, those who can't get in tend to seek universities outside the country. That is what happened to me. After some research and help from my elders, it didn't take me long to figure out that America was the right place for me to pursue my college education. I did consider other countries, but England was too expensive, and Asia didn't have enough change. America was just the right melting pot. Thirty years later, I have a greater appreciation for America because my kids don't have to leave America in search of a higher education.

Nasser began taking ESL classes, or English as a second language. Because he took the class, I figured I had to do it as well. In those days, in order to go to America, you had to pass an English proficiency test. I knew I would not have any luck entering university in Iran, so I made a point to study really hard in the English classes so I would be able to go to America. I passed, but my brother did not. I suppose this was the starting point, when I started believing that I could be better. You just have to work hard and set your mind to it. The idea of thanks to America started from that point on.

About a month before my trip to America, my father suggested that I take a few trips on my own in the country in order for me to become more independent. Though he had presented this idea as a suggestion, he had in fact arranged everything for me. He had the tickets and he knew where I would stay. My father had covered every detail of the trip.

My departure date to America soon arrived, and I was excited to be the first one in my family to go to America. It was so nice to be first in something, so it was a great day! I truly had no idea what I was up against, though. My initial purpose of going to America was to study mechanical engineering, then go back to Iran and get a good job.

At this time, the Iranian airline flew to New York. They

first flew from Iran to London, which was a nice airport but with very tight security and police with handguns everywhere. I have been back a couple of times to London since then and it is even worse now than before. I still think we really have it easy here in America compared to a lot of other places around the world. Yet, amazingly after thirty years, the Iranian airline still does not fly straight to America, even though there are almost two million Iranians in America compared to less than one hundred thousand back then.

When I was on the plane, taking off from Iran, it was in that moment that I realized what I had done. I'd left my family of nineteen years to go to a place that I only knew about from cowboy movies, soap operas, and a television show called *Little House on the Prairie*. But I knew that President Jimmy Carter was from Georgia, and that was where I was headed.

It took me a while to get myself together and face the reality. During my twenty-hour flight I noticed there were other people who were going to America for the first time, and a few of them were going to Georgia as well. Since my English was a little better than theirs, I became the spokesman for them. Perhaps that is where my leadership qualities began.

The night I arrived in Atlanta, Georgia, I checked into a motel and turned on the television set like I was used to doing at home in Iran. Within minutes it hit me. Even three years of English classes were not enough to understand the Southern English language. I had so much more to learn.

It was a very long night, but I made it to the following morning. When I got up, I looked outside and I realized how pretty Atlanta was. There were trees everywhere and it was sunny. It was February 22, 1977. And it was a great start.

# Chapter 4
## Small Gestures

"A man's true wealth hereafter is the good he does in this world to his fellow man."

-Prophet Muhammad

I was to attend Oglethorpe University, and I called my advisor, Mr. Marshall Nelson for directions. He was a nice man and made me feel that I was speaking very good English. He gave me the directions from the motel, and I got a cab for the ride to Oglethorpe.

Mr. Marshall was waiting for me when I arrived. He helped me with my bag, and he held the door open for me. This was very surprising to me. This small gesture was something that had never been done for me before. I was thinking to myself how nice he was.

While in the registration office I was told I had to pay

my school fees. I had been taught that America was a dangerous place, so my mother had sewn secret hiding places in my jacket where I kept my money. I excused myself from the registration office and went into the bathroom to get my money. Everybody laughed when they found out where I had hidden my money.

What I found so interesting by this point was that everybody I had been in contact with since that morning, from the motel clerk to the cab driver to the Oglethorpe registration staff, treated me like I was somebody important and that was a great feeling. I had never experienced that before.

I continued to learn more English as a second language at Oglethorpe University, and I lived in the dormitory and ate in the cafeteria. It was a great life and I gained weight that I still have yet to lose, yet it is the right weight for me at this time. In America watch out what you eat or it will stay with you! I enjoyed the dormitory life. It was quite new to me and very interesting. The girls and the guys shared the same campus, and that in itself was a learning experience. In Iran, universities did not provide coed campuses for the students.

Since learning English was my biggest priority, I decided not to speak Farsi, the Persian language I grew up with. I would act like I was somebody from Latin America around my Iranian friends. But about three months later, one of my Iranian friends came to my room and noticed my holy book, the *Qur'an,* which was at my bedside. The word got out, but it really helped in the early days to learn better English. My Iranian friends appreciated it as well because it helped them to practice their English. As the saying goes, when in Rome, do as the Romans do. So we did. We spoke English, we watched American movies and sports, we dated beautiful American girls, and we learned the culture as the days went on.

I always liked sports, and running was one of my favorites. Since I could not afford a car, I would run or walk to wherever I needed to go. Georgia was very beautiful with lots of trees and I was new to Atlanta so it was a win-win situation. It was good for my health and my wallet since I was on a very tight budget.

As the months went by I noticed my hair was getting long and I needed a haircut. I walked to a nearby salon and asked the cost for a haircut. The cost was six dollars. I knew that was a lot more than I could afford, and much more than the fifty cents I was used to paying for a haircut in Iran. So I bought a pair of scissors and began cutting my own hair. I became so good at cutting my own hair that my friends asked me to cut their hair. I gave them a good discount. Instead of six dollars, I charged them three dollars. It was a nice weekend income. And it paved the way for me to become what I am today.

# Chapter 5
## Thinking Big

"The highest reward for a person's toil is not what they get for it, but what they become by it."

-John Ruskin

After finishing at Oglethorpe University for English language, I decided to go to a two-year college instead of a four-year college so I could save money. I had originally planned to go to the Georgia Institute of Technology, but instead I started at DeKalb Central, which is now known as Perimeter College. But, again, because of my financial situation, I had to look for a job. I did not want to ask my father for money because I knew how hard it would be for him, especially now that he was retired and the revolution in Iran had begun.

On one hot summer day, I went in search of a job. I got

on my bike and rode along Memorial Drive, where I still like to visit at times. After quite a few hours and no prospects, I was finally hired at a pizza parlor.

I started as a dishwasher as my first job at the pizza parlor since I had done plenty of that back at home with my mother's training. It was a good job and something I knew how to do. As time went on I was promoted to other positions. I made pizza, answered the telephones, and took care of the customers and their challenges. I was so good at my responsibilities that on most nights my manager would leave the shop to me. After almost a year, I asked my manger for another raise because I thought I was underpaid. Unfortunately, he said he couldn't give me another raise because I had just received one not too long ago. I decided to quit my job thinking the manager would call me and beg me to come back to work. Well, this did not happen. It shouldn't have been a surprise, but it taught me one of my first true lessons in America.

After a few days went by, I went back to the pizza parlor on a Friday night, the busiest night of the week, only to see that the manager had replaced me with two guys. And business was booming. They didn't look like they were missing me at all. I learned from that experience that good systems run the company, not people. With good systems you will have good people.

After the pizza parlor experience, it became harder to get a job because of the revolution in Iran. Being from Iran was not that hot anymore. When we are young and not experienced enough, we tend to be, generally speaking, fairweather fans. Meaning, whichever way the wind blows or ideas come from, we will be affected by it in some shape or form. For the first two years of my life in America, the news about Iran was overall very positive, and Iranians were greatly respected as a result. Because of this, getting a

20

job, having friends, finding a roommate to share expenses with, and going to college were very easy. That was until the hostage crisis in 1979, where fifty-two Americans were held hostage in the American embassy in Iran. All of a sudden it was like night and day. My hat's off to all those Iranians who lived during those tough times in America and all over the world, and to those who lost their lives because of it. Living through those hard times caused many hardships for a majority of Iranians living abroad. Now, Iranians live all over the world. I am sure for those who are seeking to live outside of Iran it is much easier to do so as a result of more than four million Iranians living elsewhere.

I eventually found a job working as a night clerk at a 7-Eleven store. My shift was a reverse of the name; I worked from 11:00 p.m. to 7:00 a.m. Obviously, this job was not very popular because of the hours, but I needed it to pay my way through school and to make a living.

As you might imagine, there is not much business at night in a convenience store, and not much for the night clerk to do. One night after finishing my assigned job duties, I realized I still had quite a few hours until the end of my shift, and I was becoming very sleepy. I decided to straighten up the storage room and cooler, something else I was really good at from growing up at home. My mother always praised me for how good a job I did at cleaning my room, and keeping the back room nice and organized. So I got busy and started cleaning.

I'll never forget when my manager came to work the next morning. He went into the back room as usual probably thinking how he would have to push himself through the door and walk into a room that was a disaster. But, all of a sudden, he stood there rubbing his eyes to make sure he was not dreaming, and looking at a newly cleaned office where he could easily sit and count his money and do his paperwork. There was also a nice clean floor that he could eat off of. He looked at me with surprise, and I pointed him toward the cooler. He was again surprised to see everything stacked in order and properly displayed. I remember him saying, "Wow, this cooler looks so big and roomy." He was so pleased with what I had done that he called his supervisor to come and see the changes too.

It didn't take long before I was promoted to the store manager. I recall one day working hard to prepare our store for a visit from the regional manager. I had made sure that the store was organized and clean. While the regional manager was at the store, a customer emptied the trash from his car onto the parking lot before entering the store. Before I had a chance to clean up the trash, my regional manager told me to take care of the customer at the cash register and he'd clean up the trash from the parking lot. This was very inspiring to me. How somebody that high up in the company would make such a great gesture.

The lesson I learned here was that you should never ask anything of anybody that you are not willing to do yourself. Over the years of owning my own business, I have used this philosophy and my managers and co-workers live by it as well.

From time to time, the store would have sales on certain products. At this time, our promotional sale was a drink called the Big Gulp. Our job was to up-sell the bigger drink over the smaller one since it was a better value for customers and more profit for the store. At first every time our supervisor came in he would say, "Joey, think big." Meaning: sell more drinks. The prize for the contest was a microwave oven. Since I was trying to prove myself to my supervisor, I made a point to sell as many Big Gulps as possible. And guess what? My store won the competition.

The lesson I learned from that was probably one of the

best lessons in my life. Because, even though my store was low in traffic, I was able to win the contest, and that made me set my goals at a higher level from that point on. When I look back, it is amazing how that small step or victory could lead me to where I am today. I learned that when you think big, big things will happen. When you set your goals low, or if you have low expectations, usually the outcome will be low as well. I could definitely see my life in America change, thinking big and smiling are two of the main reasons why I am where I am today.

A couple of years into the job at the 7-Eleven store, I had gone out of town with my girlfriend and wasn't able to deposit the store's cash at the bank. That was cause for demotion in my title to assistant manager, and it lowered my pay. I quit my job.

A lesson I learned here was to always make your business deposits daily. And never mix business with pleasure. But, I also learned a third, and most important lesson from this. I learned that change could be a good thing. And because of it, I started to look at my life more seriously. I was twenty three years old and school was going very slowly. I had to make a commitment to a career.

# Chapter 6
## Joseph and Friends

"People deal too much with the negative, with what is wrong. Why not try and see positive things, to just touch those things and make them bloom?"

-Thich Nhat Hanh

I had been cutting people's hair on the side for the last few years, and had built up a good following. My girl-friend's mother was a successful hairdresser, and she motivated me to choose hairdressing as a fulltime career. I decided to go to hairdressing school.

I recall when I told my father about my career decision to become a hairdresser. I remember him asking me, "Why did you have to go all the way to America to learn hairdressing?" He was very upset. He said, "You could have learned cosmetology here and not wasted your time by going to the United States." Maybe his reaction had something to do with me wanting to prove him wrong, and working harder than anyone else.

Iranians are very smart and eager to learn new things, and they are inventive and original. There is a thousand years of history, and at times we are overly educated. I think sometimes that is what gets us into trouble. In fact, we feel we know everything, kind of like in the movie *My Big Fat Greek Wedding* when the father thought everything originated from Greece. Or maybe it could be the fault of the demoralizing wars between the Romans and the Persian Empire, which shifted the balance of power between the rivals.

While going to school for hairdressing, I attempted a few other ventures like part-time modeling and working as a dance instructor. There was also door-to-door sales and when I worked as an inventory clerk. But mostly, I went to school during the day, and at night I worked as a waiter in a restaurant. This proved to be a great way to meet more people and learn more about the American culture. And, it helped me to get more clients.

One night while I was working at the restaurant, one of my regular customers pulled me aside and said, "Joey, you work very hard and you attend to every detail very promptly, but I never see you smile." He told me to lighten up and take it easy. "If you smile," he said, "I am sure it will help your tips as well." That was a light bulb going off in my head. Culturally, it was something I was not accustomed to. But what a difference this simple gesture has made in my life. It definitely takes fewer muscles to smile than to frown, and it keeps me younger and keeps my banker happier.

While at hairdressing school, a professional beauty consultant had come to talk about our industry. He saw that I had great potential and suggested I apply for work at one of the high-end salons in the Buckhead area of Atlanta. I soon began work at the William's Salon on Pharr Road. William, who was from New York and Vidal Sassoon-trained, took me under his wing and taught me a lot of great things. And it was there that one of William's clients suggested I change my name from Joe to Joseph. I accepted that change because I thought Joseph was much better suited for what I was going to be doing for the rest of my life.

It is such an honor working in the beauty industry, and working at William's was a great beginning for me. I was exposed to some of the greatest people in the hair industry: Edwin and Debra Neill, Horst Rechelbacher, Scott Cole, Van Council, Don Shaw, David Wagner, and so many more. Thanks to all those I've had the fortune to meet over the years.

In order to prove to others that I was a good stylist, I entered hair competitions. After winning several competitions, one of the judges offered me a job at one of her salons. This was Betty Butler, bless her soul. It was a hard decision for me to leave William's, but I had to do it. After all, change is good.

It was a new salon in Alpharetta, and I had a great feeling about this job. Every day I got busier and busier. Of course, there are always those who can't stand to see someone else succeed, or a client who is not happy, but I loved my job and every challenge was a motivating factor for me to do a better job the next time. Hairdressing requires long hours of standing on your feet and, since I was fit by playing soccer, I was able to help my career by that.

After a couple of years working for Betty Butler, it was time to move on again. I was offered the chance to open a new salon with one of my clients, and I was excited. But eventually I had to turn her down because she wanted to bring in a third partner. I soon accepted another offer to work with Carry, who used to work with me at Betty's, and had just opened a salon down the street.

Eventually, I was encouraged by my wife and family to open my own salon, which I really wasn't sure I wanted to do because of the responsibilities. But my wife got her license in skin and nail care, and, because the owners could not make a go of it, the space for the salon I was earlier offered a partnership with had become available again. With the help of my family, my brother, Nasser, and my dear wife, Behnaz, the first Joseph and Friends was opened in June of 1989.

# Chapter 7
## The Importance of Family

"I will remember always that marriage, like life, is a journey - not a destination - and that its treasures are found not just at the end but all along the way."

-Anonymous

My wife and I had only been married a year when we opened our salon. I knew it was not going to be easy. We were working from 8:00 a.m. to 8:00 p.m., Monday through Saturday, and on Sunday we cleaned and did miscellaneous duties for the salon. It was hard on our marriage.

My wife I love very much. She is very intelligent, warm, and loves sports. She has worked very hard in order for our salon to be successful, and she has helped me to be calm and collective in discipline.

I think of marriage just like I think of business. I never take anything for granted, and I work on it every day. I have learned to be a better listener, thanks to my wife, and she has allowed me to make mistakes, and she has humbled me by her forgiveness. Just like America, she has been a great influence in my success, as a husband, father, friend, and businessman.

While growing up, my mom and dad would fight once in a while. I am sure that is probably very common in a lot of families. But I prefer more of a peaceful life, and I am the type of man who doesn't like to fight about every little thing. I am more of a free-spirit. So, because of this, I had decided that I would never marry anyone, and would not consider having children.

Well, that was my intention. As I grew older my thinking changed, and I got married and have two great kids, whom I am very proud of. Having kids is like living your life all over again. As kids grow, it reminds you of when you were a kid. Thanks to my wife who led me in that direction and always prompted me to do different activities with my children. A lot of people are afraid of having kids due to financial commitments, and I have to admit that was my fear as well. But there is a magical force out there when you decide to do something, and if you go for it with a positive attitude, God will take care of the rest and everything will be all right.

Family is important in so many aspects of our lives, but ultimately it is the safety and the security they give us. The push we need to go ahead with something. Or the encouragement we need when we fail. And our families can say so much about us as people, too. When we see politicians in public, most times they will have their families with them. We believe people that have families are more reliable and have more integrity. What does it say about the man that never shows his wife or children? Our world should be family-oriented.

When I was young, my mom used to take me and my brothers and sister to the *hammam*, which is a large Persian bath that was very common in the old days. This bathroom was big enough to fit a family of four to six, and we would all bathe together. We loved to eat pomegranates, and because pomegranates are a little messy to eat, my mom would bring them to the *hammam* with us and we would eat them there. What a great fruit. I really enjoyed the experience. I still to this day eat pomegranates.

Enjoy your kids. Those who get to see their grandchildren enjoy this journey multiple times. Help them to be what they want to be, not what you want. Practice good behavior in all aspects of your life, and let your kids make mistakes and be there for support. After all, that is how we learn. Some of the greatest inventions have been discovered by someone making a mistake. I remember in one of my classes in college my professor said, if you don't ask your question, no matter how stupid that question might be, not asking is more stupid. If you don't ask, you don't learn. Any question or mistake could lead you into a new venture. So ask as many questions and "Just Do It" because nobody is going to hold it against you. You would never know if you didn't do it!

# Chapter 8
## Karma

"Life is not easy for any of us. But what of that? We must have perseverance and above all confidence in ourselves. We must believe that we are gifted for something and that this thing must be attained."

-Marie Curie

Something that was often done in the hair industry was to shop around for stylists, and I once hired a stylist from another local shop, which was a big mistake. As you may know, hiring someone without his or her employer's permission is not good karma. So after the first few years, I made the decision to only hire people that were just out of hairdressing school or from out of town. We now do not hire anybody from a competitor unless we have permission from their employer, and their blessing. Today, with my team, we travel all over America to recruit the finest hairdressers for the Joseph and Friends Salons.

Recently, one of my employees decided to leave our company to work for another salon. Since over the years our company has been cheated by employees who left us to work for other competing salons, we decided to add a non-compete clause to our employment applications. As I was doing a client's hair one day, she began telling me about how she is waiting for a certain time period to end so she can work for another doctor. I asked why she was waiting, and she told me she had signed a non-compete agreement, and that she was honoring that agreement. As she was talking, my employee that was planning on leaving had been listening, so I made a point of saying, thank God there are still people that honor their contracts.

Don't do to others what you don't want done to you. Maybe we have not paid our dues back yet fully, and this is why I was not going to fight the employee leaving, even though I could have been successful in court. I would rather spend my time and energy on all the right things that are working in our business at this time. What goes around comes around. I truly believe in that. And, as God closes one door another door opens for you, and for some mysterious reason the next one is always better.

Early on in our business, my wife and I had only one employee. We worked every day except Sunday. We made a great income, but we had no life outside the business. We worked together and we took work home together. I remember on the first day of business, I was opening boxes of products to be put on the shelves, and I cut my finger really badly. It was on my right hand, my haircutting hand. That was the first sign or alarm of fear when I realized that I was getting into a business. If anything should happen to me, how would I continue the business? There were bills to pay and people that depended on the business. I worried that I was not going to enjoy cutting hair like I used to because of all the responsibility that goes with being an owner of a business. But my hand healed up pretty fast, and I stopped worrying, and I was able to continue cutting hair.

As our business starting taking off, I realized that I needed to have a full-time manager, especially since my wife was thinking about having children. My wife's sister-in-law, Mechelle, was a hairdresser in Chattanooga, Tennessee, so I asked her to join our team, and I asked her husband, my brother-in-law Matthew, to manage the salon. They worked with us for ten years.

Dr. Massoud is a friend I met through my wife. I like him a lot and have great respect for him. One day, while he was at my salon getting his hair cut, he noticed that I was very upset and he asked me what was wrong. I told him that I had just found out Matthew and Mechelle are opening a new salon. Since I had just expanded to a new location, financially it is going to be very hard without them, and I am disappointed that this news is a surprise for me. Dr. Massoud told me to take it easy and not to worry, it will be okay. He advised me to help them as much as I could. Be the bigger person and life will take care of you.

At first his answer was hard to swallow, but I listened to him, and guess what? Not only did my business do better, but Matthew's salon did well also. And that goes back to the lesson that if you help enough people to achieve their goals, your goals will be met as well. Thank you, Dr. Massoud, for being a great friend. I wish you well.

The lesson learned is if I always work on the positive aspect of my business and put all my energy into that, the results will be greater. And that behavior really is something that should be practiced by most people in order to have more positive outcomes. If you wish well for others, the same will happen for you. What goes around comes around.

Business got better, and our salon got busier. I had injured my knee playing soccer and I could not stand on my feet for two months. I was cutting hair sitting on a stool. During these hard times, I realized that my business heavily relies on me, which led me to start our training program. As I remember reading in a book by Michael Gerber, keep working on your business, rather than in it. "Systemize your business in such a way that it could be replicated 5,000 times, so the 5,000$^{th}$ unit would run as smoothly as the first." (from *The E-Myth* by Michael E. Gerber.)

Thanks to the Neill Corporation and Edwin Neill (an Aveda distributor in the southeast), I attended Neill Quality College and took several classes in management and training. And I also looked around at all the successful business models everywhere. Thanks to the American system that is always willing to share and help you to succeed. You just have to ask.

My friendship with Edwin Neill, the late owner of the Neill Corporation, started in 1983 when I used to work for William's Salon. Edwin Neill was truly a visionary. He was very successful at finding good in everyone. I recall one day he came to William's salon in order to motivate and help the staff. Edwin said that if he came to our salon and wanted to get his hair cut, he would only allow three out of the twenty staff members that were attending the meeting to cut his hair. His reasoning was that three people were on time, they dressed for success, they asked questions, and their hair was fashionable. Surprisingly, I was among those three, and more surprising, each one of those three people is still doing hair today, and the rest are not (maybe in their kitchens!). Throughout our friendship, Edwin's favorite song was "Row, Row, Row Your Boat":

Row, row, row your boat,
Gently down the stream,
Merrily, merrily, merrily, merrily,
Life is but a dream.

God bless you Edwin, and thanks for all of your support and kind words.

# Chapter 9
## The CRILL Elements

"Do nothing secretly; for Time sees and hears all things, and discloses all."

-Sophocles

**W**hen half of your friends are not Americans, it is really easy to hear them say something negative about being in America. I constantly hear things like, "since my hair is black," "since I have an accent," "since I am Iranian," "since September 11," "since I am a Muslim," "since my skin is dark," "since my last name is different or hard to say." When you come to America, once you decide to live here and become an American citizen, you find out there are so many opportunities around you, and all you have to do is open your eyes. When you look around, you find out that there are people from all over the world in

America who have proven themselves and are very successful. And that is exactly what I did. I followed and learned from those who valued me as an individual and respected my hard work and creativity. I have also learned there is no room for "I can't" in my vocabulary.

I have used this same philosophy in my business, which has been cause for continuous growth. Our employees stay with us, but if they choose to leave, then come back later, we take them back. And we take our clients back as well. Even people that used to work with us, then left to open their own businesses, we have helped them as well. We have people from all over the world working for us.

What is so great about my job is that it can make a difference in how our clients feel about their looks, and I can share in their happiness. All my life I have always had an attitude of giving, and in any capacity that I could afford as long as it is right and legal.

The harder I worked, the luckier I got. I really believe that. Working hard is not supposed to be all physical. After being exposed to so many successful American companies, and setting them as role models, I have been able to pave my road to success, and the following fundamentals have been the foundation of my business.

First, you have to educate. I educated myself on all the right things that were related to my business, and I educated my employees about the vision of our company. If you let everyone know from the beginning what is coming their way, more likely there will not be any surprises to come. That has been one of the hardest tasks to implement because I was always told to work hard (not smart) and to never enter into partnerships (if partnerships were good, God would have had one). Too many hands in the pot, no open-book management, don't trust, and many more. And, I was told Iranians can't work together, which our company has proved wrong as a matter of fact. I know of so many Iranian companies owned by Iranians that employ Iranians, and they are very successful at working with each other. And I believe it is because they also have adapted to the American way of running their businesses the right way.

Also, good leadership empowers you to go beyond. I can definitely see how and why America has grown beyond because of its great leadership from the past and present, and its willingness to share its joys with other countries around the world. But to have good leadership there must be five certain elements that exist. I call these the **CRILL** elements. They are commitment, responsibility, integrity, love and passion, and leadership.

**Commitment.** Living in Atlanta, snow doesn't fall too often, but one day when it did snow I was living in a house on a hill, and I could not get my car up the hill. I decided to walk to work, which was about five miles away, because I had an appointment with one of my regular clients, Bill Pretyman. As I was walking, I saw Bill driving toward me on his way to pick me up. I thought it was amazing that Bill was reading my mind. When I asked him how he knew I would be walking to work he replied, "I trusted that you would be on your way because you have always been there for our appointments." What a great guy. He is also a very successful businessman himself, and over the years I have learned a lot from him.

The lesson I learned here that I teach my staff is if you take care of your clients, they will also take care of you, and it takes hard work and dedication on your part for your clients to feel that about you. That is commitment.

**Responsibility.** By creating the right system in our hairdressing business, and trusting that system, and by trusting and empowering our employees on regular time intervals (bench marking), we have been able to grow by double digits every year. When there is a mutual trust between you and your employees, it will also create trust between the clients and your company.

**Integrity**. I was having dinner in a restaurant one evening while I was out of town for a conference, and I sat near a table of people I did not know. To make conversation, I leaned over to a man sitting closest to me and said, "You look like a wise man. Do you have any advice you could give me?" He looked at me and answered, "If you do something and no one knows about it, it is not a sin."

Well, maybe to him, but the best way I can explain integrity is when nobody is watching you, are you doing and saying what is right? If the answer is yes, then you are on the right track. If no, even 99.9 percent of the time is bad in my opinion, then you are not acting with complete integrity. To be successful in life or business, you have to be completely honest. I recall one day at work I received a phone call, and I told my receptionist to tell the person that I was not in at the time. I did not act with integrity, and it changed what my receptionist thought of me and what I was teaching her. I think there is a song that says, someone is watching you. Yes, that could be as simple as your conscious mind, which always is in you. Please use it all the time.

**Love and Passion**. I think these words are very similar in the way they describe my attachments to my work. Without love or passion for your work, you are definitely wasting your time and others' who are dependent on you. Amazingly, I have found that like attracts like. I have people in my company that are so committed and passionate and love their work, and that has contributed to our continuous growth.

**Leadership**. Good leaders empower their supporters. This not only helps their supporters achieve their goals, but it helps the leaders achieve their own goals as well. It has been said that you can have everything in life you want if you just help enough people get what they want. One thing I have always possessed was the capacity to enjoy sharing what I have with others.

As our business grew each year, I learned by other successfully-run companies that business is not a charity, and it has to make a profit in order to be able to sustain growth and security for all the people who have a job in that business. It definitely has been one of the most challenging tasks of my career simply because growing up, I was never a person who was savvy at making a profit. I remember when I was about seven or eight years old, one of my friends asked me to put our money together and start something similar to a lemonade stand in our neighborhood to make extra money. We decided to put in about two dollars, and figured we could make around eight dollars profit by selling our merchandise. When our first customer came and asked the price of the goods, my friend told him fifty cents. I was surprised, and felt we were cheating our friends and neighbors. I told him the whole thing cost us two dollars. How could he ask so much from our friend? He replied, "I cannot have you as my partner. We will lose money with you in this business."

I have to admit that my company, even though it has made a lot of money, was not profitable for a long time. I had to fund it from my personal assets for quite some time until I was smacked on the head by my financial advisor.

## Thanks To America

For the last two years, our company is making great strides toward better profits, thanks to America and the American way of running a successful business. This allows us to sleep peacefully at night. Because of our commitment, responsibility, integrity, love and passion, and leadership, as well as the right education, we are creating a financially sound company and a better life for everyone in our company. And this in turn creates better customer service as a result.

# Chapter 10
## Fake It Until You Make It

"The person with a fixed goal, a clear picture of his desire, or an ideal always before him, causes it, through repetition, to be buried deeply in his subconscious mind and is thus enabled, thanks to its generative and sustaining power, to realize his goal in a minimum of time and with a minimum of physical effort. Just pursue the thought unceasingly. Step by step you will achieve realization, for all your faculties and powers become directed to that end."

-Claude M. Bristol

This year it will be exactly twenty years since I have been married to my wife. I was thirty-one when we got married in 1988. I was very successful at doing hair, and I was able to own a home and rental property thanks to the American system whereby you can put down a low percent to own a home. I do not think that is possible in Iran. When we decided to get married, we did not have any cash and our wedding was going to cost us twenty thousand dollars. Thanks to our home equity and VISA, I was able to borrow money, and we had a great wedding. Soon after, between me and my wife working, we were able to pay off our wedding loan. The lesson learned, if you really want something badly there is always a way for you to come up with the finances and go forward.

I remember buying my first brand new car. I used my brother as a co-signer for the loan. I paid the car loan, used the car to co-sign for the down payment of my first house, and used the equity of my first house to buy my second house, and that is how it started. I have proven myself time after time and always paid my loans, and the system has trusted me to reinvest in my business over and over ever since. The lesson learned is to start small, fulfill your commitment, enjoy the achievement, and go to the next venture, while taking baby steps along the way.

When first coming to America, most of my friends worked at restaurants, convenient stores, and in delivery services, jobs that are not normally done by Americans. Mainly, jobs that do not require an MBA! What is interesting is that these jobs were all a vehicle to our successful futures. We were able to learn the American culture and the system. Thanks to America, the majority of my friends and family are holding good jobs and making good money and living very comfortable lifestyles, though they will not admit that America had a lot to do with their success.

I remember when I was in the 11$^{th}$ grade in Iran, I was disappointed at how poor our school was at getting students accepted into the universities. I went to my father asking him to change my school to a school that had a higher acceptance at the universities. My father asked me how many students from my school went to university last year. I replied that from one hundred students only three students made it. My father answered, "Then why don't you be among the three students who make it this year?" At the time I was very disappointed at my father's reply, and, with a broken heart, I accepted his answer and continued on and made it through high school. But looking back, it made me realize that ever since, no matter what situation I have been in, I have always been among the few who have made it. Thanks to my father, who has always been a great inspiration for my success.

Yes, anybody can be successful, but it depends on where the garden is, who the gardener is, and what type of fertilizer is used. Back in Iran, I remember I wanted to work at a shoe repair store near our home for a summer job. My father said, "There is no way my son will be working at a shoe repair store." He was afraid of what people would think of that, which is totally different here in America. Here, parents encourage their children to work at an early age in order for them to have more confidence. What I have learned from this is that by allowing freedom to our children and co-workers, it will inspire them to excel in every aspect of their careers and lives. In short, everybody has a vision, and I like to be a small part of their success in leading them to their ultimate vision and goal.

As one of my friends and co-workers, Raffal, used to say, "Think of me as a book and open me anytime you wish, and if I don't have the answer I will find someone who does." After all, this is America. Having good friends is essential to anybody's success. Surround yourself with good people, especially positive-minded ones. Friends that make you laugh and who support you in times of trouble, friends that can travel with you, and friends that support your ideas and give you feedback. Living in America for over thirty years, I have been very fortunate in finding some of the best friends anybody could ask for, both at work and outside my job. That is one of the main reasons I decided on the name of Joseph and Friends for my salon. No matter how good a hairdresser I was, I could not have been successful without the contributions and hard work of so many of my employees and clients, who I refer to as friends.

In my life I am always looking for signs that validate what I believe in, what I practice, and what I have done so far. One evening my wife called me into the living room to watch a documentary film called *The Secret* by Rhonda Byrne. She tells me how this documentary validates all my doing. The film talks about the law of attraction, and how by putting out only good feelings and thoughts it will get us the same in return. We attract what we are and what we think. Our thoughts, our good thoughts, can attract whatever it is we want, be it riches, fame, or good health.

It had just been a few weeks into my marriage when one morning my wife asked me to cook her breakfast. I don't know what got into my head, but I told her I didn't feel very well, and asked if she would cook breakfast for me instead. In a way, I think I was trying to make her feel bad for me so she would cook the breakfast, but in doing so, and convincing her I was not feeling well, I really did get sick. And for the first time in my career as a hairdresser, I had to call in sick to work. I could not work that day.

While faking being sick, I realized how I was able to manipulate my own health as a result. After my made-up sickness, I no longer tell anyone that I don't feel good, and thank God, or maybe thanks to my new attitude, I have not missed a day of work due to sickness since. I now see how much power we have as individuals over our own health and well-being. For the same reason, I don't miss my routine days of soccer or exercise because no matter what, I know I am going to feel better.

"Fake it until you make it." I don't know when I first heard that phrase or who I heard it from or where it originated, but I think it was when I worked in a restaurant. Since we served customers, we needed to be sure that we were creating a great experience for them, no matter what kind of mood we were in. Thanks to my job as a hairdresser, it has forced me to always be in a good mood. If sometimes I am not in a good mood, just by saying that I am to the first few people that ask me in the morning, by midday I have already forgotten what the cause of my bad mood was. I truly believe that clients are not coming to our business to hear our challenges. Next time when somebody says, "how do you do?" or "how are you?" tell them that you are doing great and no matter how bad you feel at the beginning of the day, you will be better by midday.

Try it, it works. After all, you are still alive (if you are reading this), and as long as you are alive you can do something about it.

Yes, I have always been a dreamer and a goal-setter, and I am always looking ahead because I want there to be a better tomorrow. One thing that I like to say is that I practice only to compete with myself, and I tell my employees to only compete with themselves as well. Improve daily, and don't be focused on what other people have as far as possessions and such. Only learn from them, especially the good habits. When you compete with yourself, you not only can't blame anybody else for your mistakes or failures, but you also don't risk making anybody mad by getting ahead of them. I think it is much easier to blame yourself because you can do something about it and improve yourself. You can have the control. If I blame someone else, they can't do anything about it or usually don't care to.

Staying in control is important, and I always know I am in control because I know my SWOT Analysis. SWOT stands for strengths, weaknesses, opportunities, and threats, and a SWOT Analysis is a planning tool that helps anyone evaluate their strengths, weaknesses, opportunities, and threats. It is primarily a business tool, but it can be used to evaluate your personal goals as well. It can help identify any internal or external factors that are positively and negatively affecting your goals. You can learn to better identify your strengths and learn to build on them, or discover your weaknesses and how to better control them. It can also help you identify your best talents for finding a well-suited career, or possibly what you would like to major in at college. By knowing these factors, you can have a great advantage and stay in control.

Over the years I have learned that telling the truth is also the best answer to a healthy lifestyle. When you don't lie, you don't have to worry about what you reply.

Growing up, one of my favorite uncles died due to smoking, and that is probably one of the reasons I decided to never try it. One of the most frequent questions I get asked is what do I do to stay so young looking? Usually everybody thinks it is probably my job. I am sure that has a lot to do with it, but I am sure we all know a lot of hairdressers who don't look good for their ages. I would say my secret is very simple. I always make sure I do my regular exercises. And I never worry about anything that is not going to matter a year from now. Every time I go to an older person's birthday, I ask them what their secrets are, and they tell me the same things; plenty of exercise and no worries.

Living in America you are exposed to many stories of death, disaster, and catastrophe from around the world. I am fully educated in accepting that death is essential, and those of us who are chosen first are the lucky ones. It is essential for those who are left behind to understand that life is temporary, and what is ahead of us is permanent. I want whatever is written about my life, between 1957 and whenever I pass, to hopefully say I was a good contributor to the world and to our country.

What is interesting is that I am writing this chapter on my way to San Jose, California, for the funeral of a dear friend of many years.

# Chapter 11
## Change

"Change is the process by which the future invades our lives, and it is important to look at it closely, not merely from the grand perspectives of history, but also from the vantage point of the living, breathing individuals who experience it."

-Alvin Toffler

**O**ne of the first things that I learned in America was about change. Change is something that a lot of people have a fear of. Fear of change is something that holds people back from getting ahead. From early on in America, I felt good about change, coming from Tehran to Georgia. Tehran is a beautiful city in general, in a beautiful country, but America is beautiful too, plus you have freedom. This change brought with it a lot of new experiences

for me, like new foods from all over the world and expo-
sure to more languages from all over the world. It is nice to
be exposed to different cultures. This change has helped me
become more diversified, and for that reason, I have em-
ployed people from all over the world and the clients love
it.

This change in the beginning was very hard for me to
adjust to, but I believe the younger you are, the easier it is
to accept such change. Being young when I came to America opened me to welcoming change no matter how uncom-
fortable that change might be for me. I could probably
write a whole book about change when I think about it.

The quicker you welcome any change in your life, the
faster you can advance to the next level. When you resist
change, you are resisting your own progress. I have experienced great results from all the change that I have been involved in and I am always welcoming it, and this attitude
helps me learn new things. It is probably one of the reasons
why I chose hairdressing as a career. Beauty is all about
changing a person for the better. As a hairdresser, I can
make changes that help people feel good about themselves,
and in turn, that makes me feel better about myself. Such a
process is incredibly rewarding. And it is really exciting
when you treat your life the same way. I truly believe that
people who welcome change in their lives live happier and
longer as a result. Welcome change in your life and see
your life improve. "The world says you're too old to
change. God says you're never too old to become the person you were created to be." (*Truth. Seeing Black and
White in a Gray World.* Bordon Books.)

Smiling and thinking positively also keeps you younger
and helps you live longer. Early on in America, I worked
seven days a week. I hardly had a day off. If I had time off
from one job, I was working another. I worked hard, and

being away from my family didn't leave much room for smiling. But thanks to America, we have freedom for everyone here to have something to smile about.

And do not tell or show people any negative information, because it will change the way they perceive you. I think I was about ten years old when, for some reason, I had to shave a small portion of hair off the top of my head in order for a wound to heal faster. We had to go to a family gathering that day, and I was very worried what people would say about my head. Because of how particular I was about my hair, I couldn't let anybody know about the shaved portion, so I decided to keep both my hands on my head to cover it up. After a while my mom realized what I was doing. She came to me and told me that by keeping my hands on my head I was drawing more attention to myself. And she was right because by then almost everyone was asking me why I had both of my hands on top of my head. It is interesting that so many of us unknowingly tell others about our own flaws without realizing the impact.

I remember when I lived in Iran we had more days of mourning than of celebration. The calendar was filled with mourning days and mourning months. Twelve times for the death of all prophets and an entire month of *Muharram*. During three of the months of the year, it was thought to be unfavorable for weddings.

I think it is hard to cry for something that you have not personally experienced or been involved in. I know I am a very sensitive man and I have great patience for people of all origins and from all sectors. But, I personally have a hard time attaching myself to things that happened so many years ago, and with all the tampering that goes into our past history. I can only believe what I see and what I have experienced in my fifty years of living on this beautiful planet called Earth. I truly believe that in order to have progress in any environment you have to create a happy atmosphere first.

Hope and religion are very similar. Having hope and religion are two of the most essential elements in our lives. Hope comes in so many ways, like hoping to be cured of a deadly disease, and hope of someone loving us, hope of buying something new, hope of victory over something, and so on. After living in America for over thirty years, I have come to learn that by having patience, so many hopes and desires come to us, though we just have to have the patience and the want. In other words, hope and you will have it.

America gives you that right and freedom to hope. I was watching an Iranian film about a lady who could not walk, and she was cured by a devoted religious Muslim man. You know and I know that miracles like that occur not just in movies, and pertain to not just one religious group or sector. You just have to hope that you don't live somewhere that takes any similar hopes from you.

I am glad that since I have been in America, I have been exposed to so many different religions and so many different beliefs. Thanks again America for the opportunity. I am hoping one day to be able to see a mosque run like an American church, with beautiful facilities like soccer fields and basketball courts, schools for the children, a place for both worship and recreation for the entire family, a happy place. A place that the entire family can participate together: men and women and their children. No segregation of any kind. I was born Muslim and my family is Muslim and we will always be Muslim, but I would like to pave the way for a more moderate Muslim mosque and for more moderate Muslims, which I and so many other people are.

What really makes the world a better place is the variety of ethnic groups, religions, and cultures. It would be nice to learn from each other because I think we all have something good to offer, and when you put all the good together you get something great. I believe no one has the right to kill somebody's hopes, because what one person believes does not have to be what someone else believes. I do believe in one world or one country for all, with as many beliefs and religions and ideas, but with a common law regulated. I do not believe in borders or lines between countries, as those only distance us. If there were supposed to have been borders, then God would have done it for us. I do believe that the Internet will bring countries closer to each other. I like the mixing of different languages and different cultures, and that is what makes America great.

# Chapter 12
## Everything is a Remix

"I invent nothing, I rediscover."

-Auguste Rodin

**A**fter being in America for more than thirty years, and having traveled to many countries throughout the world, I have been exposed to many different cultures. I've learned also from my job and my employees' personal backgrounds. My personal experience from running a business for the last twenty years has taught me that there are many similarities between business and politics. I think America has a great way of attracting talent from all around the world, and then allowing those people the opportunities to grow and prosper. If a person who is given an opportunity has any kind of appreciation and integrity, not only will the world benefit from that, but the people around that person will benefit as well.

My view of politics might seem too simple or too naïve, or better said, too full of wishful thinking. But I also believe that my thoughts are not original. I am sure that these thoughts have originated from many sources. You can use your own imagination here: singers like John Lennon, who sang "And the world will live as one" in his song, "Imagine"; or one world with many faces, ideas, backgrounds, and goals.

I lived in Iran during the rule of the Shah of Iran for almost twenty years. I left two years before the revolution, so my intake of the whole story is gathered mostly from all the news from here and there. The Shah was put into power just like so many others in countries with oil or gold or something similar in value. And we expected him to cooperate by pumping oil in return for a better system and other essentials, like the five CRILL elements, which these countries are in desperate need of. What happened is simple. After several years, the Shah was led to believe that Iran could operate this system alone and did not need a middle man. I can see that as a result, people of these countries have suffered time after time because they feel they can't trust America to help them.

The same mistake is made in the business I am in. If these countries shared their wealth just like America does, and cooperated with the people who live there, everyone would have better lives. This leads me to believe if they start trusting the quality of life that is enjoyed in America, it could happen anywhere in the world if greed didn't exist. I guess what I am saying is simple: Just like my business, by trusting the American system we have done better. So what if we pay taxes? So what if we have financial advisors? So what . . . ?

It is best to look at how beautiful our churches are, and

how many stadiums we have or how many great airports we have, and how easy it is to rent a car, and the many other options that are in close reach. When you are with people who think big, as a result you start thinking big. By supporting and cooperating with America's way of life, everyone wins. Let's not forget that America is a melting pot of all different nationalities and already has proven itself. Why try to recreate the wheel? It is already here. Let's be part of the solution, not part of the problem. I hope one day we all can say, "What have I done for the world?" And not, "What has the world done for me?" I can see America as one thousand states instead of fifty.

Everything in life is remixed. Nothing is new anymore. Everything is created from another idea that happened before. Take cars, for example. They all have wheels and are all built from the same fundamental concept, but with different presentations. This leads me to a story from my school days.

I was not good at drawing pictures of flowers so I would find someone who was good at it and copy his or her work. I would make it a little bigger or smaller and create a better presentation. I would make an A on my drawing, but the person that I copied from would make a B, which made them really mad. When you think about it, the flower was created by God, then humans, or a student, would draw from it or copy what God created, and somebody was mad at me because I copied theirs.

The lesson I learned was if I can't do something, I find someone else who can, hire them, and let them do the job. Why should I do it when someone else can do it better? The conclusion here is don't get selfish with your ideas. Share your ideas because nobody can do it exactly like you anyway. And that is what makes us all very unique individuals. So remix as much as you can. That is what makes the world go around much better. This is also called delegation. Become a better delegator. In Iran, this would be considered stealing or taking advantage, but in America it is called being resourceful or being a promoter or delegator.

# Chapter 13
## Choices

"We need to teach the next generation of children from day one that they are responsible for their lives. Mankind's greatest gift, also its greatest curse, is that we have free choice. We can make our choices built from love or from fear."

-Elizabeth Kubler-Ross

**W**hat goes around comes around. I was probably about sixteen years old and, enjoying soccer so much, I became a ball boy for our local soccer games in Iran. It was a great experience and I was exposed to so many soccer balls. One day I decided to keep one of the balls for myself. Twenty years later when I had to return to Iran for a visit, I took a soccer ball to play with with my old buddies at that same soccer stadium. It wasn't long before we had started the game that the ball was kicked out of the stadium, and taken by somebody who thought just like I had twenty years earlier. What was interesting was that even though I had changed my ways of doing things, I still paid a price for my indiscretion and proved the saying, "what goes around comes around."

Life is about making all the right choices. Think of a bowl of fruit with a full variety in it. Depending on what time of the day, or after what meal, certain fruits are going to taste better. So it is our choice and experience that helps us choose the right fruit for the right time of day. It is the same thing with life. The neat thing about America is that it allows us, and directs us, to make our own choices. Thanks to the forefathers of America who have paved the way for such a great country. I see that it is my duty to do the same thing for the future of our country and the world so it will be the best place for all to live.

Living in America for the last thirty years, I have realized why so many Iranians that came out of Iran are experiencing difficulty with their identity. For example, we say we are Persian not Iranian (maybe because it sounds like we are from Paris or Parisian!). Or I am Italian or Greek because these countries have better relationships with America. When I came to America in 1977, I remember when people would find out where I was from they usually were very nice to me and supportive. Dating an American girl or having friends was very easy, especially having dark hair and dark eyes. Iran was well respected among the whole world.

The first two years living in America was great. After that, sometimes I think it might have been a survival factor that made me fake my identity, changing my name from Khosrow to Joseph. The food, the language, watching American sports and movies, and basically, when in Rome do as the Romans do. It definitely worked out, but what I am thankful to America for is that it has allowed me to also enjoy some of the heritage that I come from. In America, I am able to watch over twenty Iranian television stations, enjoy many Iranian restaurants, buy any Iranian delicacy I wish, and I am allowed to exercise my Muslim faith freely. I have also learned that I don't have to fake my identity anymore. And I am respected for who I am and where I am from thanks to the President of the United States, who made a speech in support of the Iranians who live here and the fact that we can enjoy our heritage freely in a different country.

I think it is really amazing to watch any Iranian television show or go to a soccer game with my wife or daughter, or go to an Iranian party and not be afraid of anybody disrupting your party and taking you to jail and giving you one hundred slashes. I have always admired people from India for supporting their identity and being true to their heritage. That is what makes America great, that people from all over the world can come and live here, and are able to follow the news from their country from satellite television and radio without censorship and limitations, and be able to have almost anything that is from their country.

My generation in America has learned a great deal of lessons. I learned how to survive through some of the hardest conditions, and I learned to overcome my fear of rejection and failure. I learned to trust my instincts. I learned I didn't have to lie to get ahead. I learned I can be myself. I learned that the more I share my vision, my knowledge, and inspire others, the more I get help as well. I learned you can have everything in life you want if you will just help enough people get what they want.

Again, I really see that in America it is all aspects of the great American life. The society here really helps people from all over the world get what they want. Again, that is why America is where it is today. Imagine if the same settings existed in Iran today. The government would help Iranians get the help they need regardless of their status or beliefs. And, in turn, the Iranians would be more indebted to the government. It is probably wishful thinking. Hopefully one day it will happen that all Iranians, regardless of their beliefs, can live under one roof and respect each other's ideas. I pray for that day to come. I think it is definitely possible because, after all, we are all Iranian, and we have a great heritage and we could overcome all of our differences and respect all of our ideas. That is something that definitely is practical in America. All the time people have a way of communicating their ideas through very peaceful solutions. It is being done here, and I can't see why it couldn't be done anywhere else. I think the Internet is going to be a great factor and facilitator of information from each other from all over the world.

# Chapter 14
## Life as Sports

"Sports serve society by providing vivid examples of excellence."

-George F. Will, 1994

I like to run and I found out that Atlanta has a 10k running race called the Peachtree Road Race. It is one of the largest 10k's in the world, and over fifty thousand people run the race annually. The first time that I ran the race was July 4, 1977, Independence Day, and I have been running in the race ever since. It is my way of showing how thankful I am for my independence in America. I have even walked the race after I had knee surgery, and when I had a hernia. And I have made it a family tradition every year with my wife and our two children running the race, and quite a few of our friends as well. I always like to run this race with my T-shirt that has the Iranian flag, and my American flag headband to show the appreciation I have as an Iranian in America. It is amazing over the years what a great response I get from the crowds who are watching the race and those who are running in it. It is really an amazing race. And afterwards, there are picnics and fireworks.

One year I did not have an entry number to the race. I decided to run the race anyway, but I was worried that I would not get my famous Peachtree Road Race T-shirt that is handed out to all the racers every year. But, amazingly, about half a mile before the race was over someone in the crowd reached out and handed me a number, saying, "Here, this is your number." It made me so happy because I was able to get my T-shirt and continue my tradition of having one from every year.

Sports is one of the great foundations of America's success. I really believe that. The whole family can be involved. There are places where you can use the same facilities and do things together. Just to name a few are swimming, dancing, tennis, and soccer. Today in Iran, men and women cannot swim together, and women are not allowed into the soccer stadiums. It is really nice that in America, I can take my family to any sporting event and enjoy it as a whole family and we can go swimming as a whole family. I think once you are exposed to these freedoms it is hard to give them up. How could you give up your family??

Since I played soccer in Iran during my high school years, I used to travel to many parts of the city, learning about the different kinds of lifestyles that were in Iran. Playing soccer has been a great passion of mine, and I think it is a great example of team work, competition, and fitness that has influenced me to be better at what I do.

What is great in America are all the different leagues

and organizations for all different age groups playing soccer throughout the year. Since I liked soccer, my wife signed me up to coach my son's soccer team, and what a great experience it was. It was one of the most amazing experiences of my life because, not only did it help me be with my son, but it helped me play the game and learn it as well. Learning to coach young children has helped me so much in running my business. One of the greatest experiences was at the end of the season, no matter what position your team ended up in, everyone on the team would get a trophy, and nobody would be left out. What a great way to encourage kids and let them know that it is all about playing the game and not about winning.

NCAA's March Madness, what a great tournament! The celebrations, the attendance, the stadiums, the entire experience is something so amazing. What great entertainment for the whole family. There is so much to learn just from this, not to mention the NFL's Super Bowl, and the World Series of Major League Baseball, NASCAR auto races, and the Masters Tournament in golf, and so many more sports that from the ground up involve the entire family.

What great sportsmanship that is displayed after the game among the winners and the losers. I love the way that the coaches and players congratulate each other after a game, whether they win or lose. It is great sportsmanship and there is always respect for each other

A majority of the sportscasters are former players themselves. Everything is a great experience, from the stadiums to the television shows and the announcers. What a great venue to learn from and model your business or your life after. Going to American sporting events has been a great influence on my life in America. Thanks for all the great memories.

I have always been amazed at how they can blow up an old stadium, and build a new one in order to provide a better experience for the fans and an attraction to bring new venues into town. Everything is focused for the growth of the future. I have modeled this for my business as well, and it has been very successful. Always improving and creating a better experience for the client.

My son said to me one day that he wanted to play on a junior varsity team instead of the varsity team. I asked him why, and he said that he just wanted to play the game, and he didn't care about which team he played for. Since he wasn't getting much playing time on the varsity team, he chose to go to the junior varsity team. This has made me believe that in the game of life, as long as you are present and willing to play, you will come out ahead.

# Chapter 15
## Living for Today

"The secret of health for both mind and body is not to mourn for the past, worry about the future, or anticipate troubles but to live in the present moment wisely and earnestly."

-Buddha

Yesterday is history and tomorrow is a mystery. Today is present. That is why we call it a gift. While living in Iran, I was always being reminded of the past. A lot of things didn't get done because of the past and being so conscious about the future. In my American life, I've learned that my Iranian past is something that I should respect, but I am not completely proud of it because in twenty-five hundred years of history the standard of living has not improved. But in America, in two-hundred and fifty years it has. If you come to America you are free to be whoever you want to be, within reason, without being looked down upon or wondered about, free to express your identity. If you go to Iran, those in power make you who they want you to be, or you strive to be someone you think you *ought* to be. Unfortunately, in the Iranian society of a third world country, we always feel that in order for us to stay in power we must destroy the people before us, or the people who don't think like us, and start all over again. While in America, they keep building on their past and diversity.

My definition of all generations depends on where you are born and where you are from and who you are surrounded by. I do agree with the definitions and descriptions of what has been said and written about the generations, but when I look at my own business, I do see that there is a discrepancy in that idea. Some of my young team members work very hard for the opportunity, and they are not waiting for a handout. I see people from overseas that see the opportunity more clearly. I also appreciate the fact that my generation who came from abroad is self-made and can form to any hard-challenging situation, and they do not give up when things go bust like the economy or stock market or real estate. And what's more, we started from nothing and we had fun while building our future, and we learned to respect our achievement and learn from our mistakes.

In life we always come across those who inspire us and mentor us. Wilson Harrell was one of those many in my life. When my business was new and struggling, one of my regular clients, Charlene Harrell, gave me a book that was written by her husband, Wilson Harrell. I read the book and some of it made sense and some of it did not. Unfortunately, I lost the book and I also lost Charlene as a client, but I didn't lose the lessons I had learned from Wilson Harrell. A few years went by until one day, while in a Serious Business conference, one of the speakers was talking about Wilson Harrell. Wilson had been a fighter pilot in World War II. He'd shot down a German plane and, as a result, he was shot down and badly burned. He was rescued by the French underground who kept him safe by burying him in a cornfield so the Germans couldn't find him. For eleven consecutive days he was buried with nothing but a hose stuck in his mouth to breathe through, while the Germans trampled over the field looking for him. It was only when the war ended that he was safe.

After his experience in the war, Wilson went on to become an entrepreneur, brilliant marketer, and a very successful businessman using those same survival skills and the keen instinct that proved so valuable in the war.

After I heard the speech from the presenter at Serious Business, I was in tears and disappointed in myself. Wilson had also made a great impact in the presenter's life, and he was disappointed because Wilson had just passed away. Sure enough I was too because he was right nearby for so many years and I had the opportunity to thank him personally for being such a great inspiration.

How my story relates to him in some shape or form is that like him, he started from nothing, and though he lived with tremendous fear while hiding from the Germans, after being freed he was not afraid of trying anything new. I believe fear is what keeps us from doing things and experiencing things. Fear of failure. Fear of rejection. Fear of those who do not approve of what we believe or do.

As soon as I got back from the conference, I called Charlene and told her about the story and asked her permission to thank Wilson in my book. Thank you Wilson Harrell, and Charlene, for helping me out when I needed it.

The lesson I learned through this was when something or somebody inspires you, recognize and appreciate them promptly.

# Chapter 16
## Trust

"When I'm trusting and being myself... everything in my life reflects this by falling into place easily, often miraculously."

-Shakti Gawain

It is the 23rd of April, Thursday around twelve-thirty in the morning. My wife is in Iran visiting her family in Tehran. I called my wife. She is going to be in Iran for about a month and she has already been there for a week. She is very happy to be there, very impressed with the brand new airport and the subway system and all the new highways, but doesn't like the busy traffic. Her mom just bought a new television, but they are having a tough time getting reception. In Iran it is hard to have a satellite system because the government does not trust their own people to make the right decisions. It has been proven the more you micro-manage people the less productive they will be. I hope this book will not prevent me from being able to travel to Iran.

One of my hopes for this book is to show that people can work together and respect each others' beliefs no matter where they are from. It is okay to disagree on certain things and ideas, and I believe that no matter what government is in charge, it should respect people with different backgrounds and beliefs. We need to be better communicators and better listeners. That is why we have one mouth, two ears, and two eyes, given by God. We should listen and watch more than we talk. This simple idea has definitely helped me in my business and in my everyday life. That is why I wanted to keep this book short and easy to understand. Living a good life and a happy life is not hard. It has been done before. Again we just have to open our eyes and listen more to those who have already done it before us.

Never blame anyone for your failure. Only you should take the full responsibility first and last. This is one thing that I really think hurts a lot of people. They always blame others for their failures, or other countries for the problems in their own countries. They ignore the fact that it might be a problem with their society or their system or their own behavior that causes the hardship. If I don't show up to work, how can I blame the owner of the shop for me not being busy? If I don't practice new haircuts, how can I blame clients for not coming to me? If I lie to my employee, how can I expect them to trust me? If I don't respect people from all different backgrounds, how can I have a successful business? If I don't create an environment for the growth of all employees at all times, how can there be any development? When there is a win-win attitude in any environment, that business or society will create a great place for everybody to prosper and grow.

One of my clients, George, was planning a trip to Dubai for business, working on a deal with a businessman from the Middle East. George told me he was not sure if he could trust this deal to go through. He thought that after the deal went through, the businessman would cancel the contract. George worried that after finding out how the product was made, the businessman would want to copy it on his own and keep all the profits, while also cutting out the middle man. This made me think; maybe this is why some countries can't have a relationship with the United States. Every time we trust someone in the Middle East, they turn on us and go back to their way of doing things. I think there is a great similarity between how we pay taxes and all the benefits we receive in return. I believe that if America can trust someone in any Middle Eastern country, we all will live a better life in return.

We just have to work on the trust factor, just like I did when I changed my way of doing things. It will take a long time, and maybe it will not be in my lifetime, but it has to start from somewhere. I think it already has started. I know many successful and trusted Middle Eastern businessmen in America, and I think it is our job to transfer this great system to other countries in need.

In Iran during my school days, I remember at exam time, teachers would watch every student like hawks so we would not attempt to cheat. And it was amazing all the creative ways in which we would try to cheat. Sometimes I say if we had spent all that time learning, we would not have had to cheat.

In my first year in America in college, I was amazed that the teacher would leave the room during exam time. Even during an open book test sometimes. The lesson I learned here was that if the teachers trust you, trust that you are a responsible adult and know better, you learn that if you cheat, you are only cheating yourself. It seems the more someone restricts you from doing something, the more you are going to try to cheat that system. And in the long run, it is the people of that country who would pay the big price; the price of not trusting one another.

On one of my recent vacations in Florida, my son asked me how I felt about leaving my business in other people's hands. I was proud to say that I felt very comfortable doing so because we have been able to create a sense of freedom, responsibility, and ownership in all of our employees, and that has created a safe environment for the employer and the employees. Thanks to America for teaching me and inspiring others to do the same. Trusting yourself to speak the truth at all times not only adds to your life but also creates a very sustainable future for everyone involved.

One great example of trust is the U.S. Soccer team. It has been able to become one of the top soccer teams in the world in a very short time, and I credit that to the management system and the trust it has had in the primary schools, the colleges, and the different leagues. Trust from the ground up. And, from recruiting some of the best talent from all over the world.

It was not yet a year that I had lived in America, and since my college and work was only a three- to five-mile walk from my apartment, and I could not afford to buy a car, I bought a bicycle and used it for all my transportation needs. Having the bike was very exciting, especially since it was the first bike I had ever owned. For safety reasons, my dad would not buy a bike for me since the traffic jams in Tehran were really bad. I still got plenty of practice though using my friend's bike.

One day, my neighbors who were also Iranian, told me that the Kmart near our apartments, which was about six miles from us, was giving away watermelon. They both went with their bikes, and each one brought back one watermelon. I got excited since I also liked watermelon, and decided to go and get the free watermelon. When I got to the Kmart, I noticed everyone picking watermelons and putting them in their cars. I decided to put my watermelons in a shopping cart. I loaded ten of them in the cart and was going to pull the cart with my bike. Then I thought of a great idea. I had a friend who worked at Kmart and was a neighbor of mine. I told him that I had these watermelons and my ride was not coming and asked if he would mind giving me a ride with my watermelons and my bike as well. Once I got back to my apartment my neighbors were upset because they hadn't thought of the same idea.

I soon left to go to work and when I returned home all my watermelons were gone. Guess who took them? Yes, my neighbors had taken all of my watermelons. I guess it is easy come, easy go, as they say.

But my real lesson came later on when I went into the Kmart to shop. I noticed that as I was checking out, somebody was paying inside for the watermelon that was on sale outside. It was embarrassing. Yes, trust. It was neat to see that there is so much trust that people would pay for one and pick one outside, or buy two and pick the melon outside.

I was very embarrassed and told the story, the true story, to my neighbor who'd given me a ride with my watermelons, and my neighbors who took the watermelons. Later on we all went back to Kmart and paid for our free watermelons. Every time I think about that story I get a chuckle out of it.

The lesson learned: nothing in life is for free because it will disappear soon if you don't earn it or pay for it.

Speaking of the bike, after having the bike for almost a

year, I was running late for a class and I decided not to lock the bike as I always would have done. And guess what? When I finished my class and went to get my bike, it was gone. It was a very sad moment because it was the only affordable vehicle for me at that time. But the good news was that it paved the way for me to save enough money and buy my first Volkswagen Super Beetle for $1,700. At twenty-one years old, I bought my first car.

America is built on trust, and that is something that I experienced as soon as I came to America. Having a great system in place early on, on all levels of life, has created such a powerful country called the United States of America. I owe my success to this great system, and I give thanks for the opportunity to be able to serve it.

# Chapter 17
## A Balanced Life

"Every now and then go away and have a little relaxation. To remain constantly at work will diminish your judgment. Go some distance away, because work will be in perspective and a lack of harmony is more readily seen."

-Leonardo DaVinci

**A**fter fifty years of my life, I have realized that there are three things that are most essential to a balanced life. They are equally important, and if you balance the three easy habits, it will pave the way for a very successful life. These are (1) sleep, (2) work, and (3) socialize. Also known as **SWS.**

**Sleep**. Sleep, as most people know, is the most essential. It is food for the body and brain, and you actually don't gain any weight if you remain at fifty-six hours a week. If you can do seven hours at night, and a one-hour nap in the middle of the day, that is even better. My mom does that and she loves it. Try it, and your mind and body will appreciate it.

**Work.** Work at least eight hours a day. Someone might say, that is fifty-six hours a week, and my answer to that is yes it is. In order to get ahead, you have to do extra and I am looking only at my own profession. From the time that I used to cut hair every day, and went to as many educational classes as I could, to now with multiple salons, I spend most of my time on developing new talent and making their dreams come true. I always tell my staff, work forty hours a week doing hair, then spend another sixteen hours a week bettering yourself by reading and practicing in job related activities.

**Socialize.** This encompasses fitness, family outings, getting together with friends, going to church or mosque, or whatever else you like. And sometimes, socialize just with yourself to reflect and gather your thoughts. Socializing means anything that fits your lifestyle. It is proven that people who have a good balance between SWS tend to live longer. So try to balance your SWS.

I don't compare myself to others or worry about what other people do or have. I do on occasion drink, but I definitely don't have to have a drink in order to have a good time. I surround myself with positive-minded friends. I never gossip or try to make somebody look bad. Being in love, loving my wife, and doing my job are other factors in my staying young, as well as having great friends. I am one of the luckiest people to have so many great friends that I can depend on to help me at anytime. Keeping educated about my job and having kids are other big factors in staying young for me. I always go and do exercises with them, and nothing is more precious than being able to go with my son to soccer practice or running with my family.

I am very visual and a good listener, and I have been for over fifty years of my life. Because of my success in the beauty industry, I have been able to travel to so many different places thanks to America. And I've been exposed to so many different cultures and customs, and it makes me believe and understand what life is really all about.

Vacationing is important. A must. It doesn't matter where you are from, you must do it. Some countries do it really right, almost the whole three months of summer. Most nations of the European Union have laws mandating a minimum of four weeks' vacation time for full-time employees, who by the way, only work thirty-five hours a week. In Japan, it is five weeks, and in Switzerland, it is six weeks. Taking a vacation is encouraged in Europe.

Early on, it was very hard for me to take any vacation. As I became more American and the longer I stayed here I became better at making time for myself, thanks to America. America provides you with so many options and choices and places to go, and at a low cost for the whole family from camping on mountains to lakes and beaches. It is amazing how easy it is to take a vacation from booking an airline ticket to renting a car. It can be done online over the Internet without having to pay anybody a bribe. And there are so many other advantages. Too many to mention that provide a wonderful experience for a great vacation, and you don't have to belong to a special group to enjoy these privileges. You can even pay for it later. "Just do it," like the Nike commercial says. Do it, and then in good faith, work to pay for it later. What a blessing we have here.

# Chapter 18
## The Turtle and the Hare

"America lives in the heart of every man everywhere who wishes to find a region where he will be free to work out his destiny as he chooses."

-Woodrow Wilson

I am sure many of you have read or heard about the race between the turtle and the hare, either in English or in your own language, and I am sure we all have our own understanding of the story. I'd like to share my understanding of what I believe the story is about with you, and hopefully one day I will read your idea of the story as well on my web site, thankstoamerica.com.

What is certain in our lives are two facts. The first fact is we are born and the second fact is we will die, and we all know these as facts of life. Now, in my version of the race story, I imagine two individuals who are born together. Let's say that's on October 7, 1957. And they live until the year 2057, hopefully. Person number one, or the turtle, which I like to believe I am, starts the race or journey by slowly looking around and using all of his five senses; seeing, touching, smelling, hearing, and tasting. Since the turtle is not concerned about the outcome, he truly enjoys the race, and his life while in the race. If you pay close enough attention you can see it in his face.

Now, the second person, or the hare, is only using two of his senses during the race; his sight and his hearing. He looks to see where the turtle is, and he gets ahead and falls asleep. Then the hare hears that the turtle is ahead of him, and starts racing. Because he is too overconfident he begins to party and doesn't pay attention to all the nice things the race has to offer. Finally, they both finish the race with the turtle finishing ahead of the hare.

The lesson learned in this story is to make sure you live your life fully and use all five of your senses. If you imagine our lives as the race and look at it as the turtle did and enjoy it fully, we will all be winners at the end of the day. As my wife's uncle, Dayee Yosef, told me on one of our trips to Florida while we were swimming, swim slowly so you can go farther by pacing yourself. Every time I hear wise advice like that I try to incorporate it into most of my doings. Thanks Dayee for your inspiring words during your trip from Europe to America. I enjoyed having you as our guest. I hope you come back soon.

What life is really all about to me is first knowing, learning, and exploring as much as we desire because knowledge is wisdom, and the wiser you are the better decisions you can make. Second, it is about doing. Mastering it. Knowing that I have the knowledge, I need to use it or practice it. So I went to school, got the knowledge and now

I am working. Use your own imagination as well. Third, it is about sharing; meaning now is the time for me to share my knowledge that I have learned throughout my life and my work experience. I need to share it with those who need it or want it. I think going through these three simple steps of life will pave the path for a complete life cycle for every person that goes through it. Do it until you make it, and then share it, teach it or be a mentor. And the sooner you get to the cycle of sharing or mentoring, the better you will become. What you learn and do may be your best, but when you share what you know and mentor others, all of a sudden it multiplies, and that is what the real secret to life is all about. The good that you do will teach others to do good as well.

What has made me want to continue living in America and not go back to Iran is the freedom. Freedom is the most important thing in any living creature's life, especially for human beings. Once you have it, you do not want to lose it. The longer I live in America, the more freedom I have. Free from a past where I was dictated to on what I was to be or believe, free from an unknown future, free from the present law that does not allow men to do hairdressing for women. Free from the doubts that kept me from attaining my goals, and hesitancy in wondering whether what I am doing is right or wrong. And free to speak or wear whatever, to do, to act, to dance.

I also feel living in America allows me the opportunity to write a book that can mentor others, especially those from Iran and other countries, and to make us known as a peace-seeking nation. Hopefully, this is not the first or last book of its kind, and I am sure there are more to come. I believe I can do more for my Iranian heritage from abroad than inside the country. I hope this book and the accompanying website is a catalyst for everyone to share and mentor more people by sharing their life experiences. For those who are thinking why thanks to America, what I'd like to propose is that you share your thanks as well. Share your thanks to America, or to the country that has enabled you to live your dream. And in the end it will be nice to see which story can inspire us the most.

Lastly, never forget what I call LASA, as spoken by the Indian guru, Sathya Sai Babam, love all, serve all. If we do nothing else but live our lives to love one another and to serve one another, we can make an enormous change in the world. We could possibly see countries get smaller and borders disappear, and end up with one world, with many faces.

# On The Cover

The art on the cover of the book is a design by graphic artist David Gaudio, depicting a pomegranate with the world's flags, an idea inspired by artists Nazanin Kani and Henrik Abedian.

The pomegranate is said to have originated in Persia, but its symbolism has been depicted in myths, legends, and religions of many different cultures for centuries. It's a symbol of fertility, wealth, and eternal life. To be buried with a pomegranate will bring rebirth, and to count the seeds fallen from inside a pomegranate will foretell many offspring.

According to the *Qur'an*, the pomegranate grows in the gardens of paradise. The Prophet Mohammed encouraged his followers to eat pomegranates, which he called "good things that God creates," to rid themselves of envy and hatred. And the seeds are a symbol of fruitfulness. We picked the image of the pomegranate to represent the world without envy and hatred. Flags appear on the fruitful seeds that spill out from the pomegranate symbolizing all the world's nations existing together peacefully and generously.

The pomegranate was and is to all a superfruit; nutritious, blessed, and propitious.